This book belongs to
_____

Wilma Rudolph

By Mary Nhin

This book is dedicated to my children - Mikey, Kobe, and Jojo.

Copyright © 2022 by Grow Grit Press LLC. All rights reserved. No part of this book may be reproduced in any form without permission in writing from the publisher. Please send bulk order requests to growgritpress@gmail.com
Paperback ISBN: 978-1-63731-795-2 Hardcover ISBN: 978-1-63731-797-6
Printed and bound in the USA. MiniMovers.tv

One unique thing about me is that I have a big family. A really, big, big family. I'm the 20th child of 22 children.

When I was a baby, I was born prematurely and my immune system was very weak.

I've had several illnesses such as pneumonia and scarlet fever. This caused me to miss kindergarten and first grade in public school, so I had to be homeschooled.

When I was five years old, I was diagnosed with polio. This made it difficult for me to walk. The doctors feared I would never walk again.

Since my legs were weak, I had to wear braces and use crutches to get around. It was hard on me, but luckily, my family was very supportive. This helped me have a fighting spirit.

Then one day, when I was 12, I was able to get my braces removed!

There was very little medical help for African Americans in the 1940s so my parents seeked help from the historically black Meharry Medical College. The medical college was 50 miles away from where we lived, but for two years, my mother and I took a bus every week to get treatment and strengthen my legs.

I made sure to walk everyday and exercise the best I could to strengthen my legs. It wasn't easy and, oftentimes, it felt impossible but I began to see progress after consistently training my legs.

My wonderful supportive family, also, massaged my legs four times a day!

I challenged my body and joined the basketball team at school. I was told that I was a very fast runner.

One day someone noticed my potential and I was asked to join the track team. This is when my track journey began. Many people doubted me because of my past struggles in life, but I didn't let that affect me. I believed in myself.

I focused only on what I could control. I practiced a lot and challenged older, more experienced athletes in hopes of improving.

I earned the nickname "Skeeter" because my coach said I was fast as a mosquito.

When I turned 14, I was invited to a track camp where I won all nine races. I loved the challenge and competition.

Winning is great, sure, but if you are really going to do something in life, the secret is learning how to lose. Nobody goes undefeated all the time. If you can pick up after a crushing defeat, and go on to win again, you are going to be a champion someday.

In my junior year of high school, I had the opportunity to attend the Olympic trials in Seattle, Washington.

Much to everyone's surprise, I qualified to compete in the 200 meter race in the summer Olympics in Australia. There were only five people that qualified for the team and I was one of them. To say I was excited was an understatement.

MELBOURNE 1956

At age 16, I was a member of the American 4x100m relay team that won the bronze medal. This only made me thirsty for more competition and I set my sights on the gold medal at the next Summer Olympics.

In 1960, at the Summer Olympics in Rome, I won gold medals in three events. I was officially proclaimed the fastest woman in the world! I became the first American woman to win three gold medals at a single Olympic Games.

After I retired from my track career, I became a second grade teacher at Cobb Elementary. I wasn't entirely out of track. I served as a track coach at the high school I attended and worked extensively with underprivileged children.

My hope is that my experiences can give hope to others battling illnesses and disabilities. There are many things you cannot control in life, but you can control your effort and work ethic.

Timeline

1945 - Wilma is diagnosed with Polio

1952 - Wilma gets leg braces removed

1956 - Wilma wins bronze medal in Summer Olympics in Australia

1960 - Wilma becomes the first woman, not to mention the first African-American woman, to win three gold medals

minimovers.tv

 @marynhin   @GrowGrit
#minimoversandshakers

 Mary Nhin   Ninja Life Hacks

 Ninja Life Hacks

 @ninjalifehacks.tv